My Process

I begin everything by hand with just a blank sheet of paper and a pencil. After capturing in pencil the shape of whatever it is that I'm going to draw, I start filling the shape in with designs in black ink. After filling in the figure with details, I scan it, and voila! Now you have a nice design to color.

My home studio has plenty of work surfaces, coloring supplies, and inspiring art to surround me while I work.

D1142963

Here I've started to fill in a design outline with details like dense stripes and circles.

A pile of finished designs.

I like to work at my sunlit desk!

About Me

My name is Valentina Harper and I grew up in Venezuela, where my childhood was filled with drawing, coloring, and painting. As an adult, I came to the United States with a brilliant imagination and a heart full of dreams. After getting a degree in graphic design and working for fifteen years as a graphic designer, I discovered a new life as a professional artist. In my Nashville studio, I spend countless happy hours playing with my paints and my pens, nurturing my world of fantasies and dreams where my uplifting drawings and designs take shape. I enjoy working with different materials, but black ink is one of my favorite mediums. My attention to intricate detail is my signature drawing style.

Basic Coloring Ideas

Now that you're familiar with the range of colors available to you, you can use many different techniques to apply color. Here are just some ideas to get you started! As you make your coloring choices, remember that everything is allowed. You can mix techniques, colors, and tools however you want to put the finishing touches on your piece. The important thing is for you to relax and enjoy the process!

Color large areas: Color each section of a drawing in one single color. There's no need to get caught up with coloring each and every little tiny shape separately if you don't want to!

Use a monochromatic color palette: Use only different shades of the same color on a design. Choose any single color (primary, secondary, or tertiary!) and play with various shades of it—for example, use different dark pinks and reds with light pinks for accents.

Alternate colors: Within each section of a design, color each small shape in alternating colors. Try using two similar colors in each section, like the light and dark pink, light and dark brown, and light and dark orange shown here.

Use shading: Within specific spaces or areas of a design, play with the intensity of the color you've chosen. Especially with tools like colored pencils, you can simply press lighter or harder with the tool to go from a lighter color to a darker color and achieve a gradient effect across an area. This can add real dimension to a coloring.

Use white space: Leave some areas of a coloring white to add a sense of space and lightness. This can work really well with light color schemes, but can also create a cool, bold effect with dark color schemes.

Tip

If you're working directly in your coloring book, take care of the book by putting a blank sheet of paper underneath it to prevent the ink from bleeding through onto the next design. You can also put a sheet of paper underneath your hand while you're coloring—this will prevent your hand from accidentally smearing the color already on your work.

© Valentina Harper, www.valentinadesign.com. From *Creative Coloring Through the Seasons* © Design Originals, www.D-Originals.com

© Valentina Harper, www.valentinadesign.com. From *Creative Coloring Through the Seasons* © Design Originals, www.D-Originals.com

© Valentina Harper, www.valentinadesign.com. From *Creative Coloring Through the Seasons* © Design Originals, www.D-Originals.com

© Valentina Harper, www.valentinadesign.com. From *Creative Coloring Through the Seasons* © Design Originals, www.D-Originals.com

© Valentina Harper, www.valentinadesign.com. From Creative Coloring Through the Seasons © Design Originals, www.D-Originals.com

Things to do this Fall

© Valentina Harper, www.valentinadesign.com. From *Creative Coloring Through the Seasons* © Design Originals, www.D-Originals.com

© Valentina Harper, www.valentinadesign.com. From *Creative Coloring Through the Seasons* © Design Originals, www.D-Originals.com

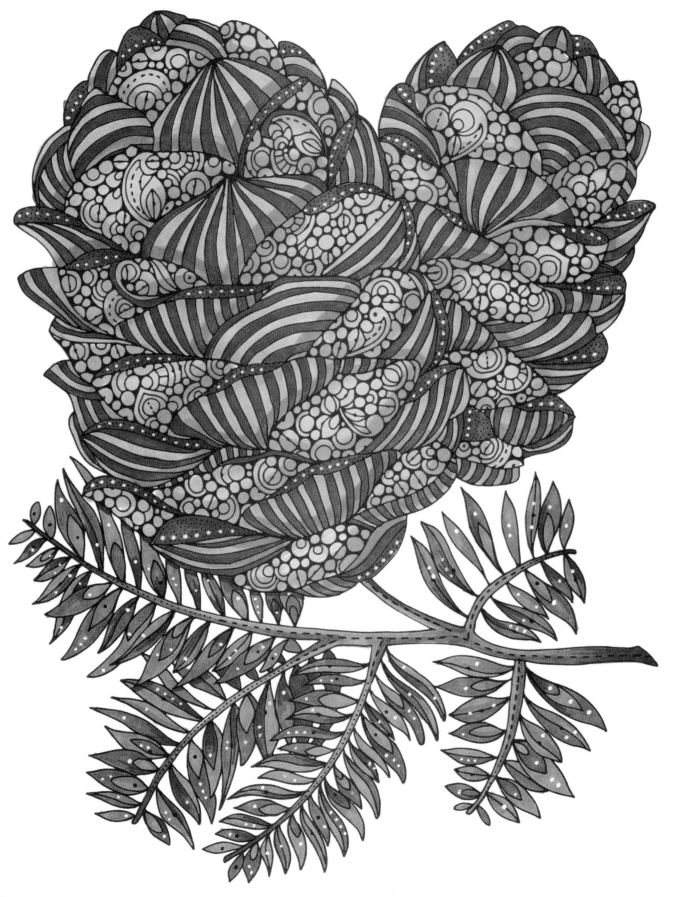

© Valentina Harper, www.valentinadesign.com. From *Creative Coloring Through the Seasons* © Design Originals, www.D-Originals.com

Summer Bucket List

© Valentina Harper, www.valentinadesign.com. From *Creative Coloring Through the Seasons* © Design Originals, www.D-Originals.com

© Valentina Harper, www.valentinadesign.com. From *Creative Coloring Through the Seasons* © Design Originals, www.D-Originals.com

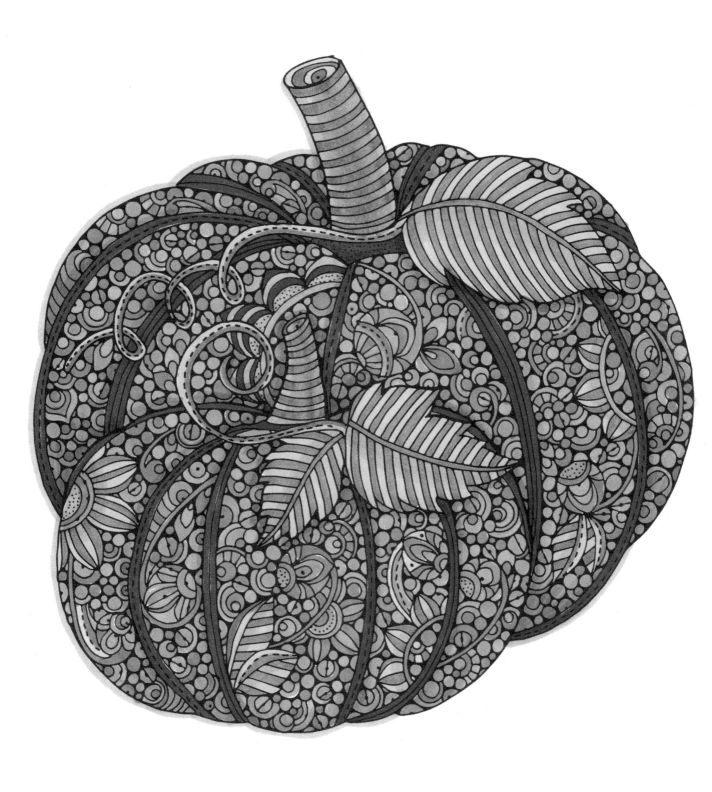

© Valentina Harper, www.valentinadesign.com. From *Creative Coloring Through the Seasons* © Design Originals, www.D-Originals.com

© Valentina Harper, www.valentinadesign.com. From *Creative Coloring Through the Seasons* © Design Originals, www.D-Originals.com

"Spring has returned.
The Earth is like a child that knows poems."

–Rainer Maria Rilke

No matter how long the winter, Spring is sure to follow

© Valentina Harper, www.valentinadesign.com. From *Creative Coloring Through the Seasons* © Design Originals, www.D-Originals.com

"In winter, I plot and plan.
In spring, I move."

–Henry Rollins

What will you do this spring?

SPRING ACTIVITIES CHECKLIST

© Valentina Harper, www.valentinadesign.com. From *Creative Coloring Through the Seasons* © Design Originals, www.D-Originals.com

© Valentina Harper, www.valentinadesign.com. From *Creative Coloring Through the Seasons* © Design Originals, www.D-Originals.com

"Write it on your heart that
every day is the best day in the year."

–Ralph Waldo Emerson

© Valentina Harper, www.valentinadesign.com. From Creative Coloring Through the Seasons © Design Originals, www.D-Originals.com

"In the spring, at the end of the day,
you should smell like dirt."

–Margaret Atwood

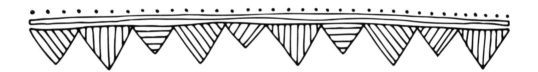

© Valentina Harper, www.valentinadesign.com. From *Creative Coloring Through the Seasons* © Design Originals, www.D-Originals.com

Add your own patterns to the Easter eggs.

© Valentina Harper, *www.valentinadesign.com*. From *Creative Coloring Through the Seasons* © Design Originals, *www.D-Originals.com*

"Spring won't let me stay in
this house any longer!
I must get out and breathe
the air deeply again."

–Gustave Mahler

© Valentina Harper, www.valentinadesign.com. From *Creative Coloring Through the Seasons* © Design Originals, www.D-Originals.com

"The beautiful spring came;
and when Nature resumes her loveliness,
the human soul is apt to revive also."

–Harriet Ann Jacobs

© Valentina Harper, www.valentinadesign.com. From *Creative Coloring Through the Seasons* © Design Originals, www.D-Originals.com

© Valentina Harper, www.valentinadesign.com. From *Creative Coloring Through the Seasons* © Design Originals, www.D-Originals.com

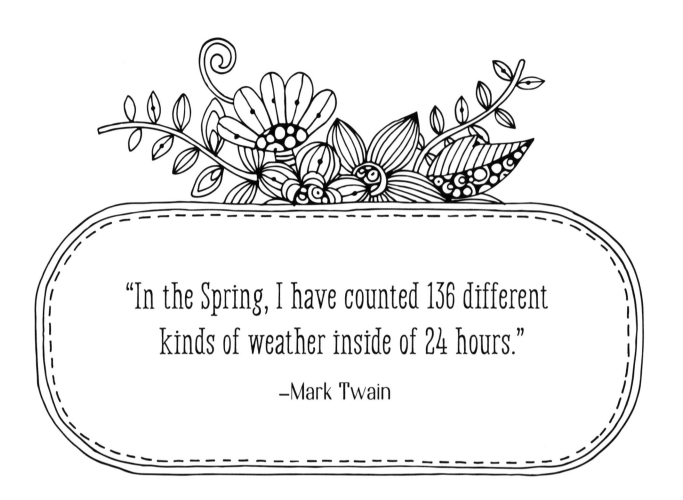

"In the Spring, I have counted 136 different kinds of weather inside of 24 hours."

–Mark Twain

© Valentina Harper, www.valentinadesign.com. From *Creative Coloring Through the Seasons* © Design Originals, www.D-Originals.com

Draw more flowers to complete the garden.

© Valentina Harper, www.valentinadesign.com. From *Creative Coloring Through the Seasons* © Design Originals, www.D-Originals.com

"At the Summer Solstice, all is green and growing, potential coming into being, the miracle of manifestation painted large on the canvas of awareness."

–Gary Zukav

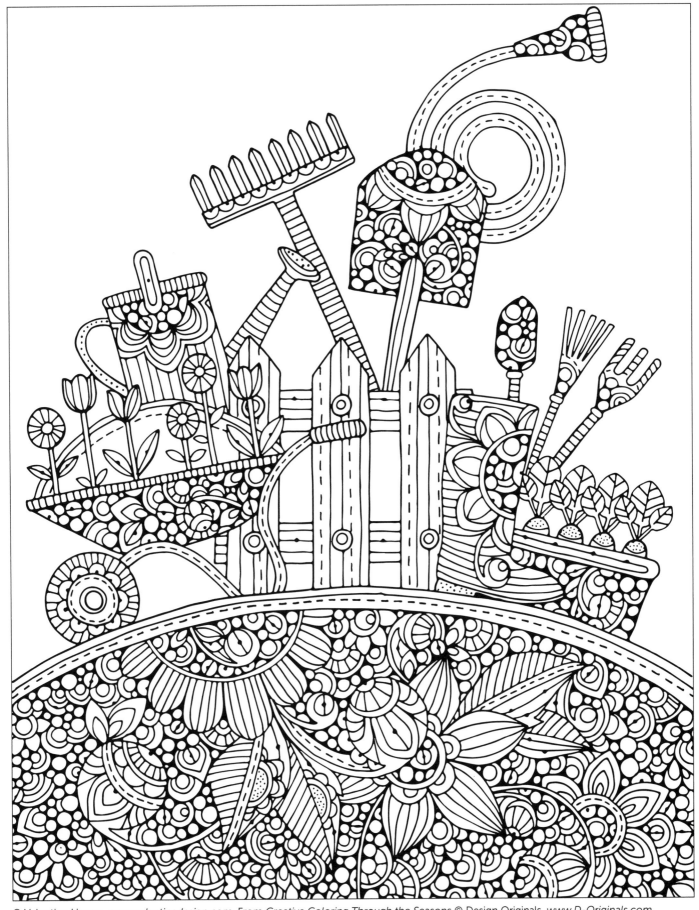

© Valentina Harper, www.valentinadesign.com. From *Creative Coloring Through the Seasons* © Design Originals, www.D-Originals.com

© Valentina Harper, www.valentinadesign.com. From *Creative Coloring Through the Seasons* © Design Originals, www.D-Originals.com

"Summer is the annual permission slip to be lazy.
To do nothing and have it count for something.
To lie in the grass and count the stars.
To sit on a branch and study the clouds."

–Regina Brett

What will you do this summer?

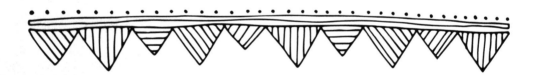

Summer Bucket List

© Valentina Harper, www.valentinadesign.com. From *Creative Coloring Through the Seasons* © Design Originals, www.D-Originals.com

"To escape and sit quietly on the beach—
that's my idea of paradise."

–Emilia Wickstead

© Valentina Harper, www.valentinadesign.com. From *Creative Coloring Through the Seasons* © Design Originals, www.D-Originals.com

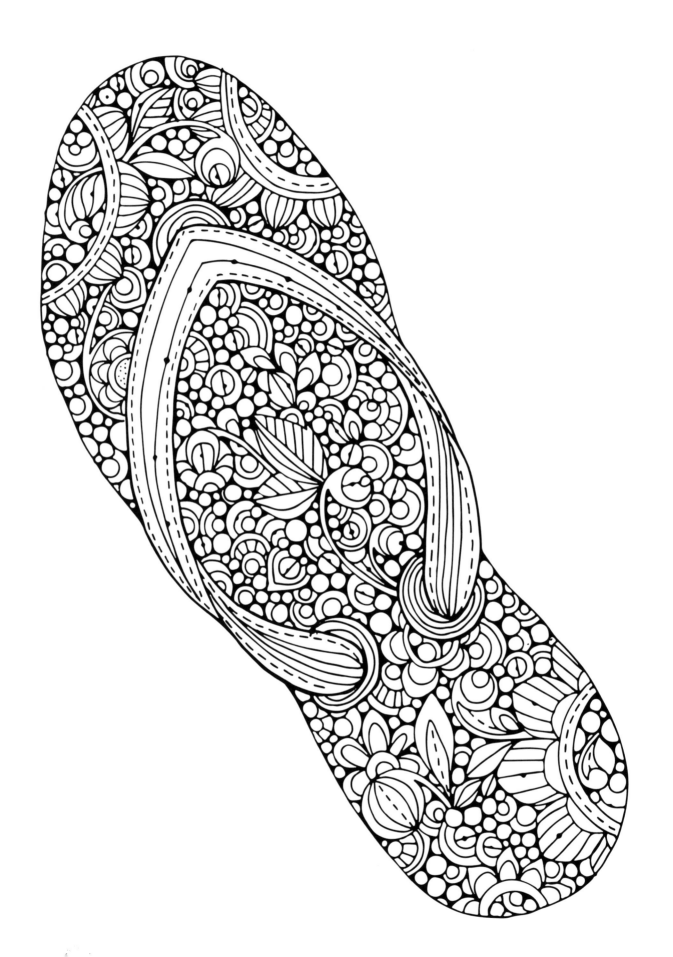

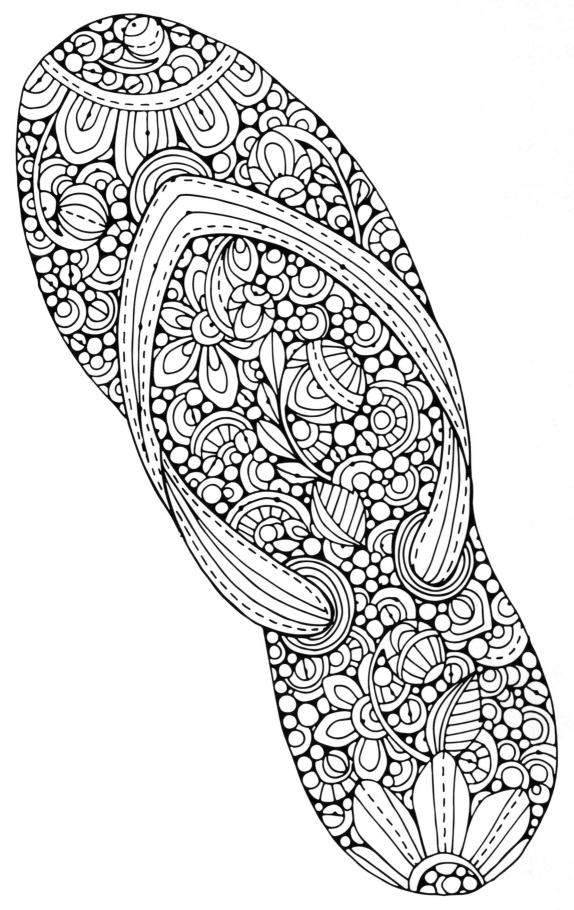

© Valentina Harper, www.valentinadesign.com. From *Creative Coloring Through the Seasons* © Design Originals, www.D-Originals.com

"Keep close to Nature's heart . . .
and break clear away, once in awhile,
and climb a mountain or spend a week in
the woods. Wash your spirit clean."

–John Muir

© Valentina Harper, www.valentinadesign.com. From *Creative Coloring Through the Seasons* © Design Originals, www.D-Originals.com

HELLO
Summer

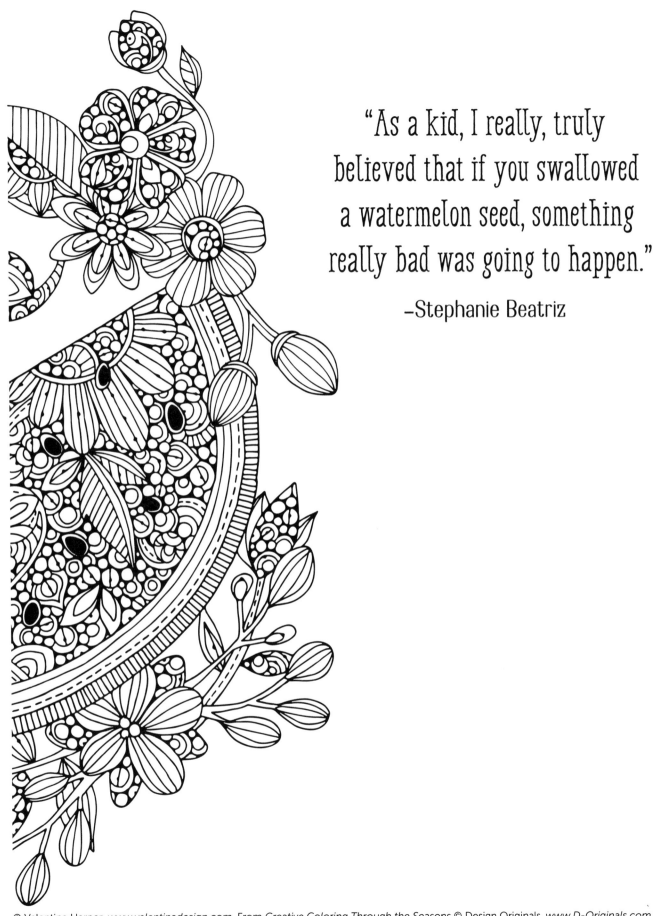

"As a kid, I really, truly believed that if you swallowed a watermelon seed, something really bad was going to happen."

–Stephanie Beatriz

© Valentina Harper, www.valentinadesign.com. From Creative Coloring Through the Seasons © Design Originals, www.D-Originals.com

"Summer afternoon, summer afternoon;
to me those have always been the two most
beautiful words in the English language."

–Henry James

© Valentina Harper, www.valentinadesign.com. From *Creative Coloring Through the Seasons* © Design Originals, www.D-Originals.com

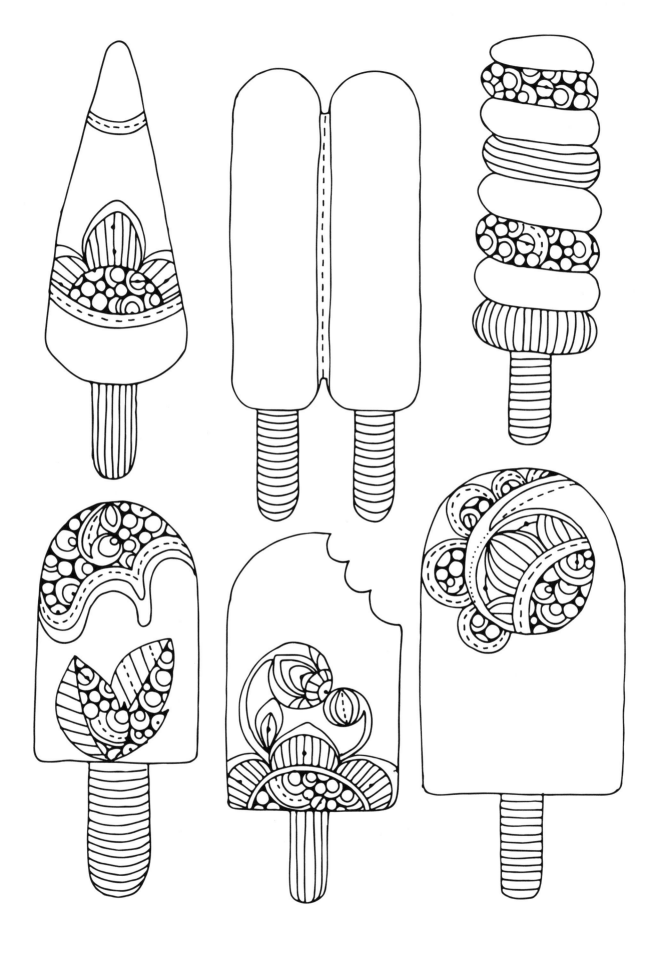

stay cool

COMPLETE THE DESIGNS

© Valentina Harper, www.valentinadesign.com. From *Creative Coloring Through the Seasons* © Design Originals, www.D-Originals.com

"A tree is known by its fruit; a man by his deeds. A good deed is never lost; he who sows courtesy reaps friendship, and he who plants kindness gathers love."

–Saint Basil

© Valentina Harper, www.valentinadesign.com. From *Creative Coloring Through the Seasons* © Design Originals, www.D-Originals.com

"Look deep into nature, and then you will understand everything better."

–Albert Einstein

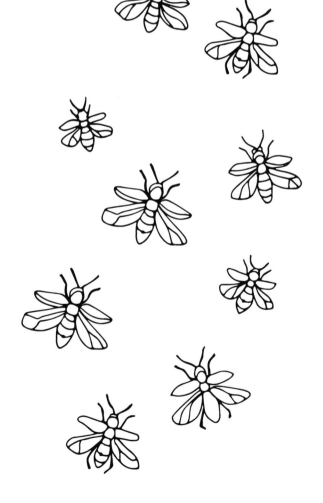

© Valentina Harper, www.valentinadesign.com. From *Creative Coloring Through the Seasons* © Design Originals, www.D-Originals.com

Complete the design.

© Valentina Harper, www.valentinadesign.com. From *Creative Coloring Through the Seasons* © Design Originals, www.D-Originals.com

"Deep summer is when laziness
finds respectability."

–Sam Keen

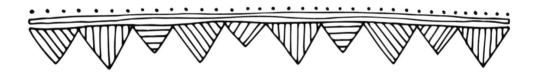

TAKE ME WHERE
summer
NEVER ENDS

© Valentina Harper, www.valentinadesign.com. From *Creative Coloring Through the Seasons* © Design Originals, www.D-Originals.com

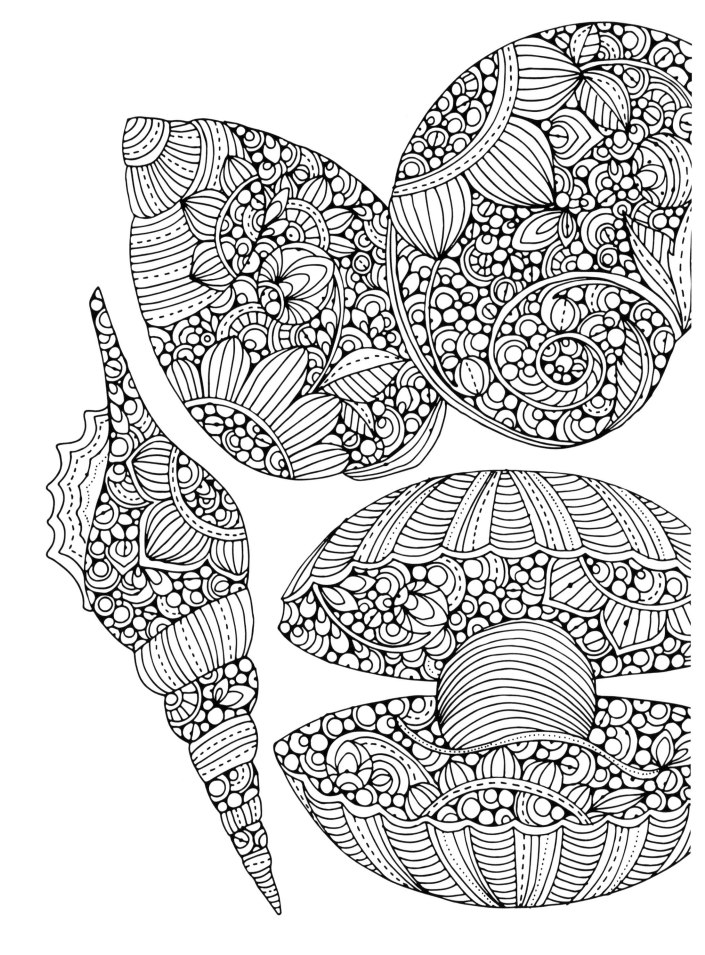

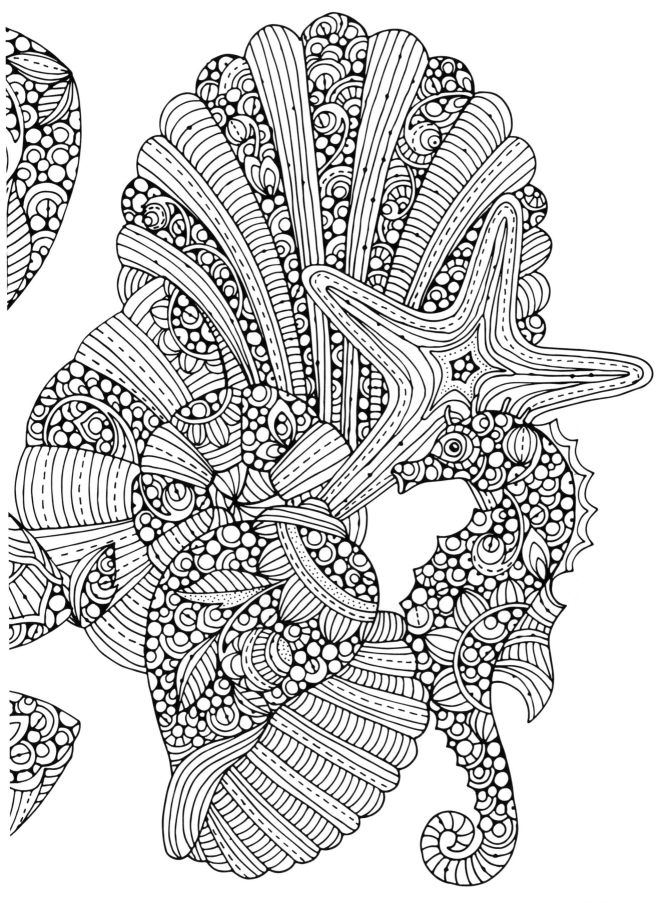

© Valentina Harper, www.valentinadesign.com. From *Creative Coloring Through the Seasons* © Design Originals, www.D-Originals.com

"I know that if odour were visible,
as color is, I'd see the summer garden
in rainbow clouds."

–Robert Bridges

© Valentina Harper, www.valentinadesign.com. From *Creative Coloring Through the Seasons* © Design Originals, www.D-Originals.com

"There is a time in the last few days of summer when the ripeness of autumn fills the air."

–Rudolfo Anaya

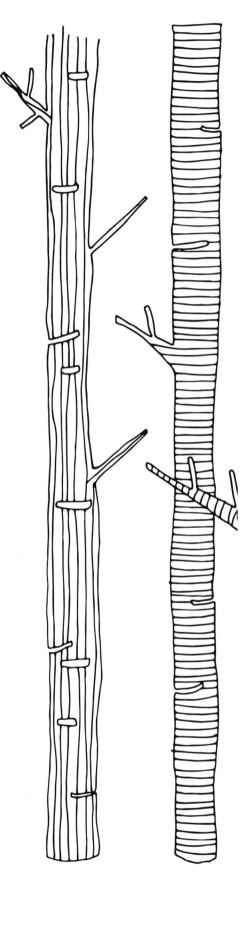

© Valentina Harper, www.valentinadesign.com. From *Creative Coloring Through the Seasons* © Design Originals, www.D-Originals.com

"By all these lovely tokens
September days are here,
With summer's best of weather
And autumn's best of cheer."

–Helen Hunt Jackson

© Valentina Harper, www.valentinadesign.com. From *Creative Coloring Through the Seasons* © Design Originals, www.D-Originals.com

Make your own designs in the leaves.

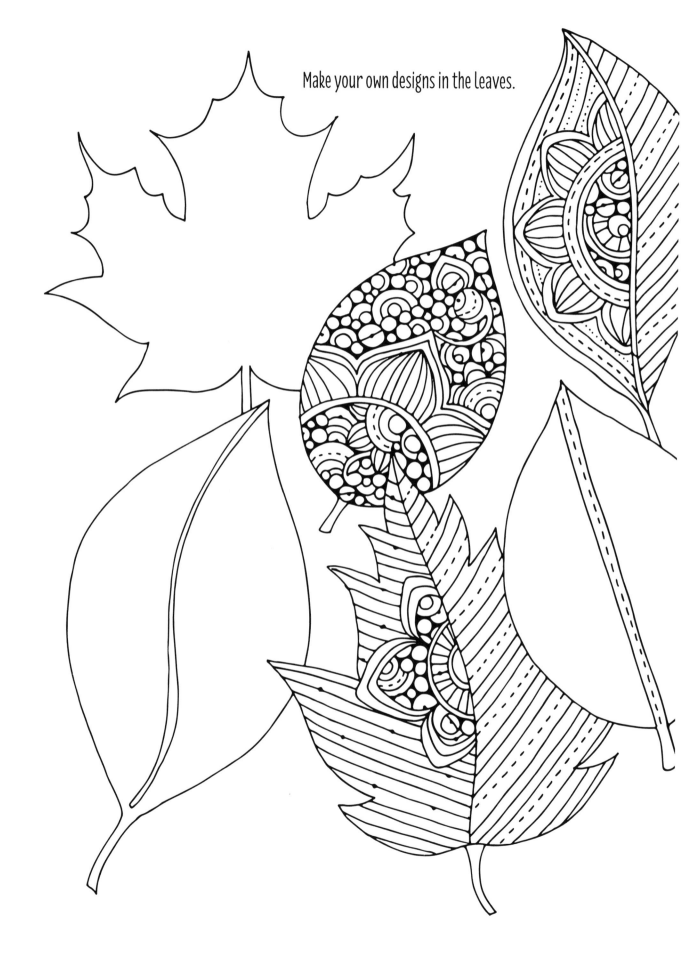

© Valentina Harper, www.valentinadesign.com. From *Creative Coloring Through the Seasons* © Design Originals, www.D-Originals.com

"It is only the farmer who faithfully plants seeds in Spring, who reaps a harvest in the Autumn."

–B.C. Forbes

What are your fall goals?

Things to do this Fall

© Valentina Harper, www.valentinadesign.com. From *Creative Coloring Through the Seasons* © Design Originals, www.D-Originals.com

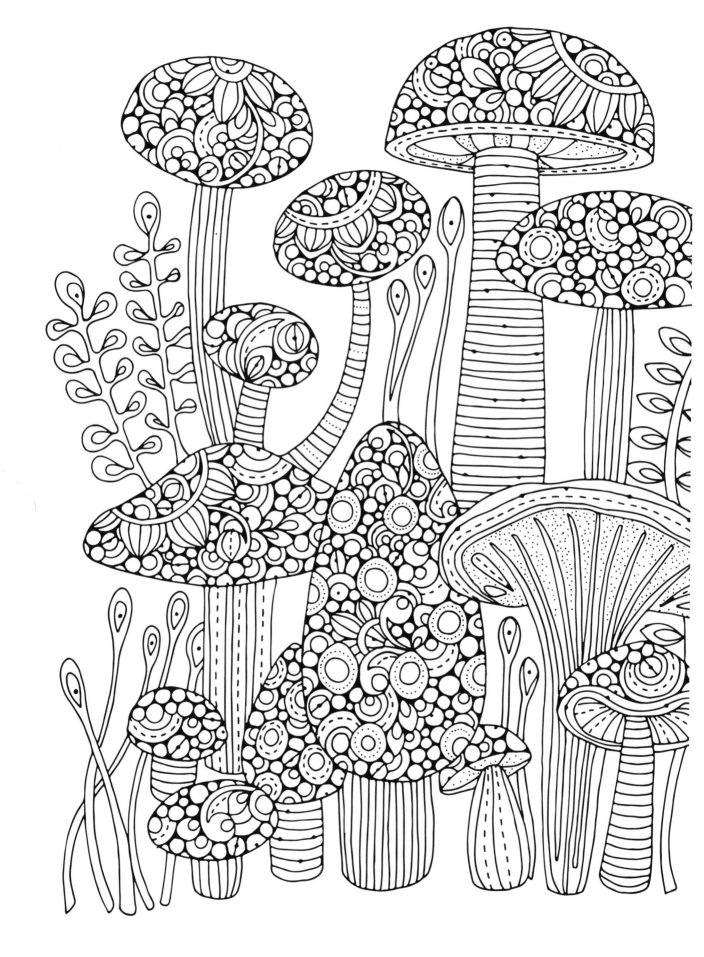

© Valentina Harper, www.valentinadesign.com. From *Creative Coloring Through the Seasons* © Design Originals, www.D-Originals.com

"Delicious autumn!
My very soul is wedded to it,
and if I were a bird I would fly about the
earth seeking the successive autumns."

–George Eliot

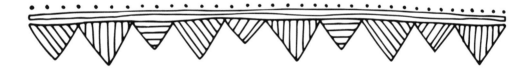

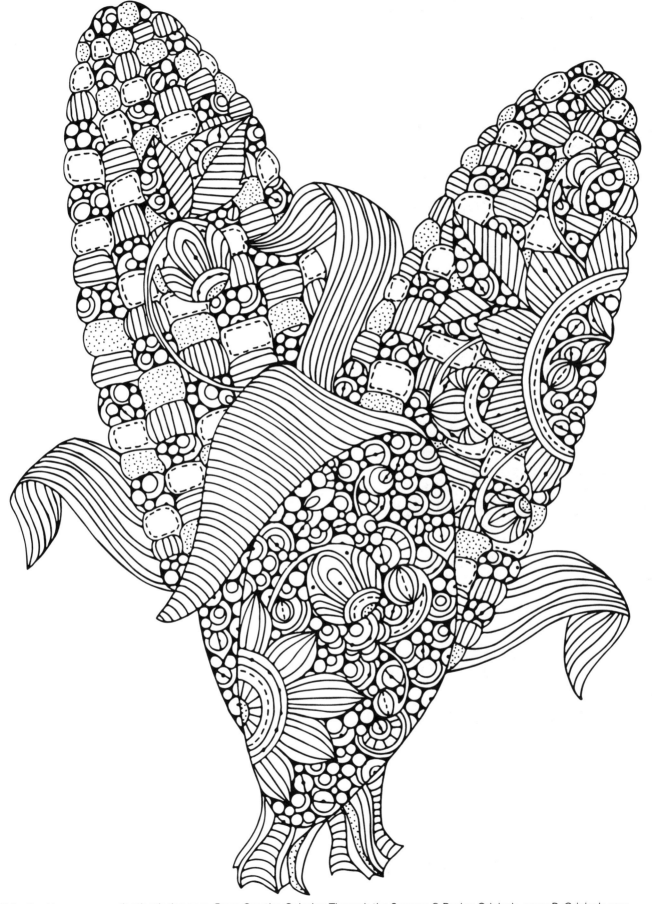

© Valentina Harper, www.valentinadesign.com. From *Creative Coloring Through the Seasons* © Design Originals, www.D-Originals.com

© Valentina Harper, www.valentinadesign.com. From *Creative Coloring Through the Seasons* © Design Originals, www.D-Originals.com

"Autumn is a second spring
when every leaf is a flower."

–Albert Camus

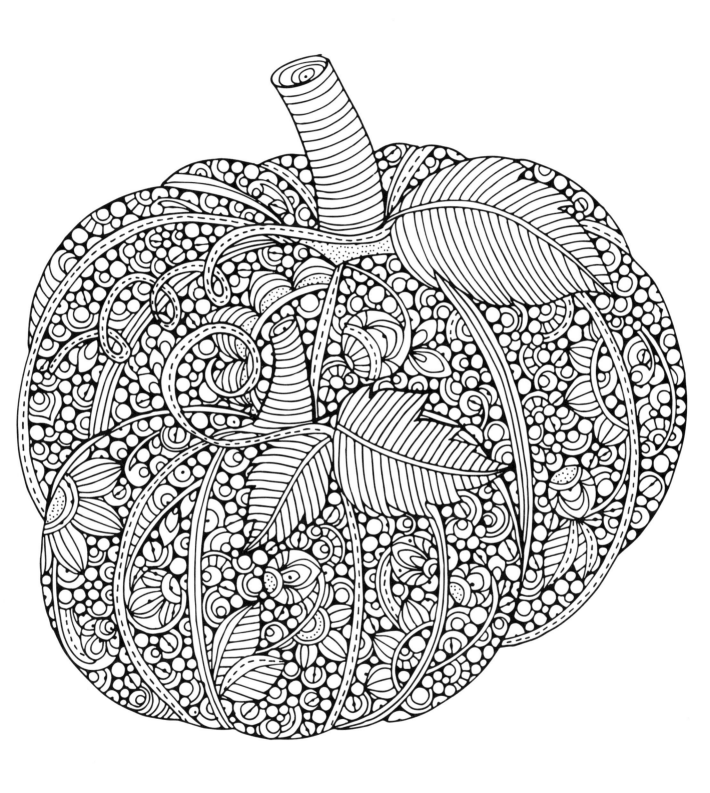

© Valentina Harper, www.valentinadesign.com. From *Creative Coloring Through the Seasons* © Design Originals, www.D-Originals.com

"Nature's beauty is a gift that
cultivates appreciation and gratitude."

–Louie Schwartzberg

© Valentina Harper, www.valentinadesign.com. From *Creative Coloring Through the Seasons* © Design Originals, www.D-Originals.com

© Valentina Harper, www.valentinadesign.com. From *Creative Coloring Through the Seasons* © Design Originals, www.D-Originals.com

"When the seasons shift, even the subtle beginning,
the scent of a promised change, I feel something stir inside me.
Hopefulness? Gratitude? Openness? Whatever it is, it's welcome."

–Kristin Armstrong

© Valentina Harper, www.valentinadesign.com. From *Creative Coloring Through the Seasons* © Design Originals, www.D-Originals.com

"Sometimes we should express our
gratitude for the small and simple things like
the scent of the rain, the taste of your favorite food,
or the sound of a loved one's voice."

—Joseph B. Wirthlin

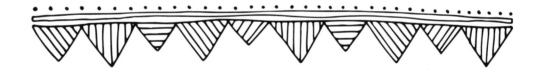

I'M THANKFUL FOR:

© Valentina Harper, www.valentinadesign.com. From *Creative Coloring Through the Seasons* © Design Originals, www.D-Originals.com

"Love is a fruit in season at all times,
and within reach of every hand."

–Mother Teresa

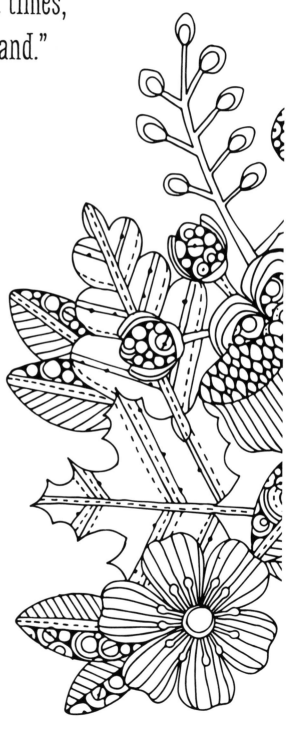

© Valentina Harper, www.valentinadesign.com. From *Creative Coloring Through the Seasons* © Design Originals, www.D-Originals.com

"The spirit of Christmas is the spirit of love and of generosity and of goodness. It illuminates the picture window of the soul, and we look out upon the world's busy life and become more interested in people than in things."

–Thomas S. Monson

© Valentina Harper, www.valentinadesign.com. From *Creative Coloring Through the Seasons* © Design Originals, www.D-Originals.com

"Christmas is a bridge.
We need bridges as the river of time flows past.
Today's Christmas should mean creating happy hours
for tomorrow and reliving those of yesteraday."

–Gladys Taber

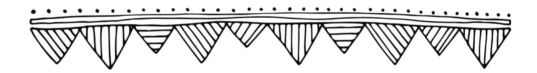

© Valentina Harper, www.valentinadesign.com. From *Creative Coloring Through the Seasons* © Design Originals, www.D-Originals.com

© Valentina Harper, www.valentinadesign.com. From *Creative Coloring Through the Seasons* © Design Originals, www.D-Originals.com

"Winter is a season of recovery and preparation."

–Paul Theroux

What are your goals for this winter?

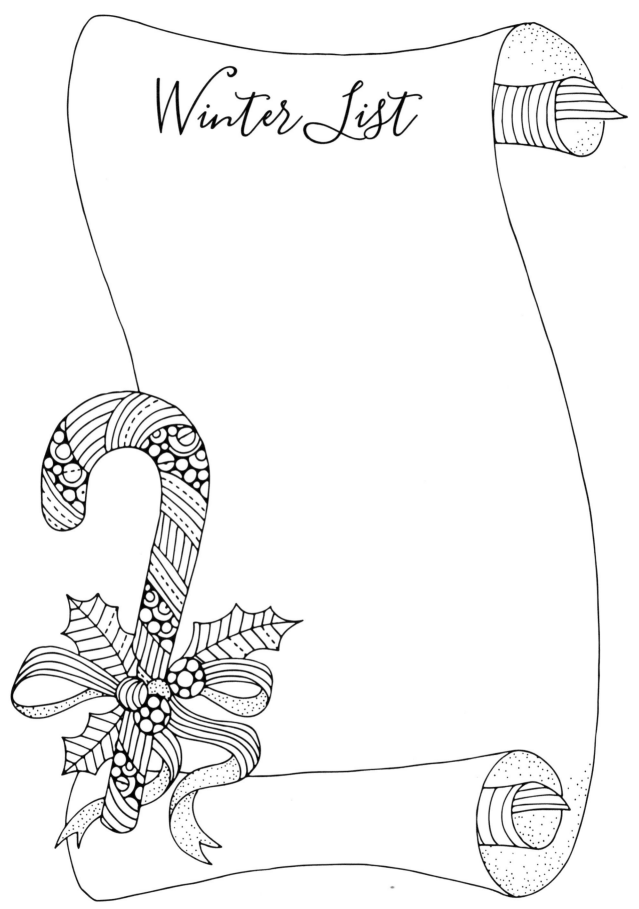

Winter List

© Valentina Harper, www.valentinadesign.com. From *Creative Coloring Through the Seasons* © Design Originals, www.D-Originals.com

COMPLETE YOUR
Stocking

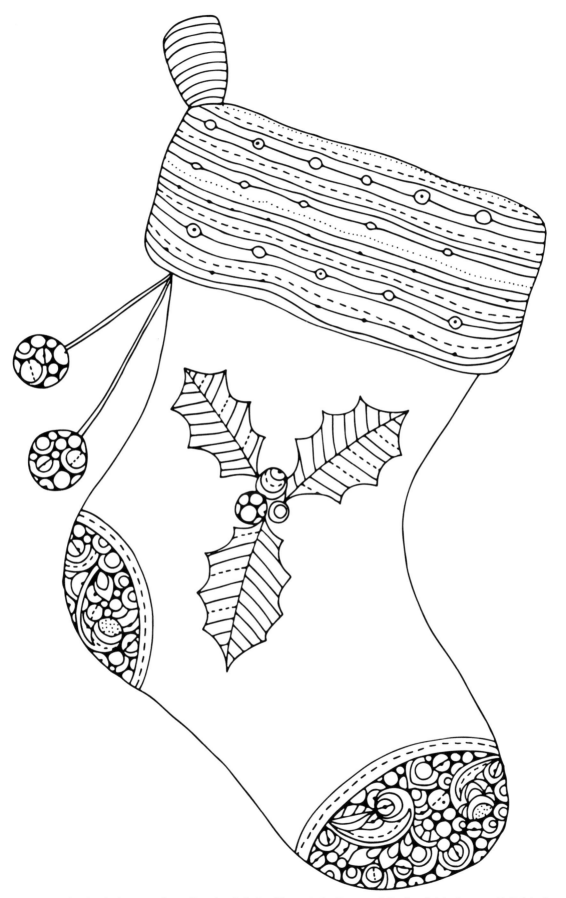

© Valentina Harper, www.valentinadesign.com. From *Creative Coloring Through the Seasons* © Design Originals, www.D-Originals.com

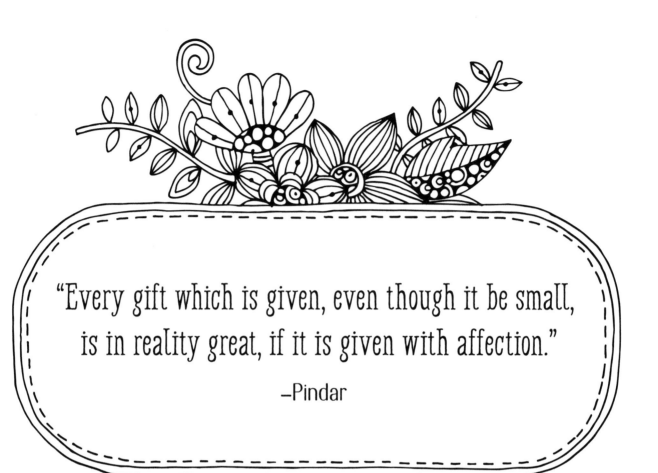

"Every gift which is given, even though it be small,
is in reality great, if it is given with affection."

–Pindar

© Valentina Harper, www.valentinadesign.com. From *Creative Coloring Through the Seasons* © Design Originals, www.D-Originals.com

"He who marvels at the beauty of
the world in summer will find equal cause
for wonder and admiration in winter."

–John Burroughs

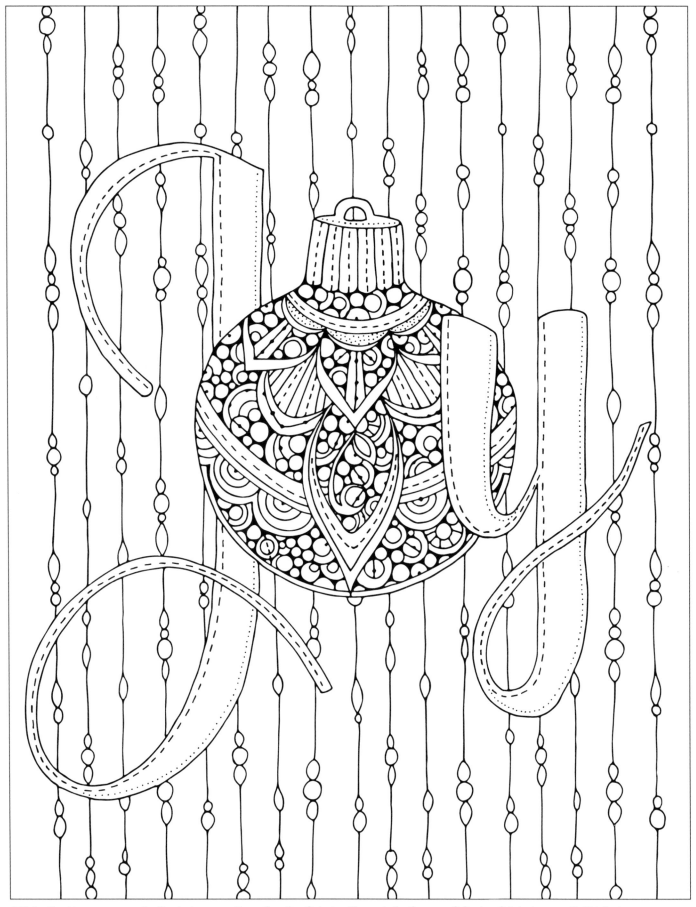

© Valentina Harper, www.valentinadesign.com. From *Creative Coloring Through the Seasons* © Design Originals, www.D-Originals.com

NOW DESIGN ONE FOR A FRIEND

© Valentina Harper, www.valentinadesign.com. From *Creative Coloring Through the Seasons* © Design Originals, www.D-Originals.com

"My heart is like a singing bird."

–Christina Rossetti

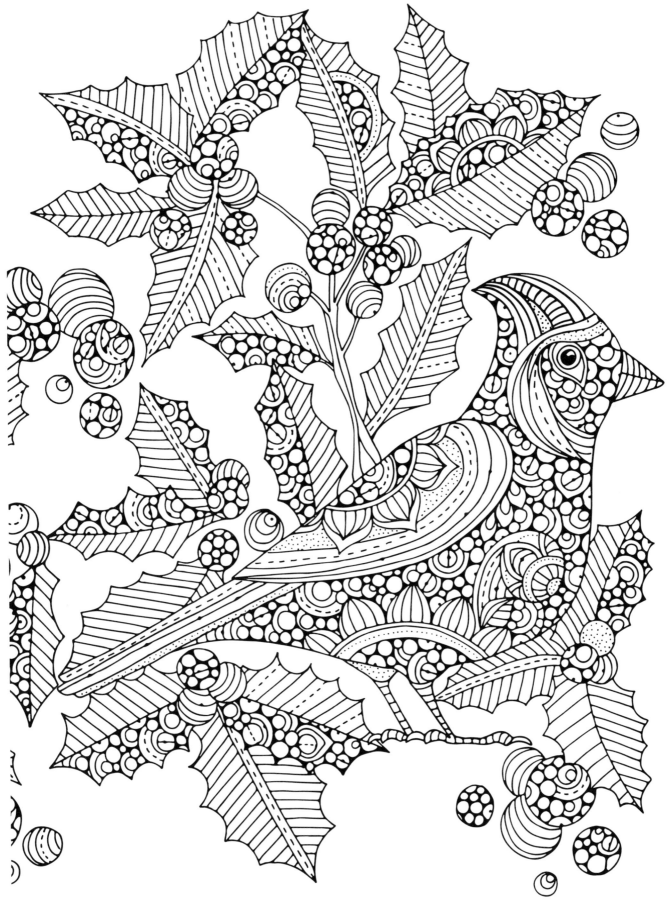

© Valentina Harper, www.valentinadesign.com. From *Creative Coloring Through the Seasons* © Design Originals, www.D-Originals.com

"The first fall of snow is not only an event,
it is a magical event. You go to bed in one kind of world
and wake up in another quite different, and if this is
not enchantment then where is it to be found?"

–J.B. Priestley

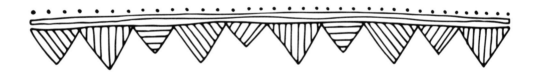

© Valentina Harper, www.valentinadesign.com. From *Creative Coloring Through the Seasons* © Design Originals, www.D-Originals.com